How Can I Be Healthy?

Alcohol

Sarah Ridley

W

FRANKLIN WATTS
LONDON•SYDNEY

First published in 2010 by Franklin Watts

338 Euston Road, London NW1 3BH

Franklin Watts Australia

Level 17/207 Kent Street

Sydney NSW 2000

Series editor: Melanie Palmer

Text: Sarah Ridley

Designed by: Pewter Design Associates

Series design: Peter Scoulding

How Can I Be Healthy? is based on the series *It's Your Health*

text © Jillian Powell 2004

ISBN 978 0 7496 9588 0

Illustration: Mike Atkinson and Guy Smith, Mainline Design

Picture researcher: Diana Morris

Series consultant: Wendy Anthony, Health Education Unit, Education Service, Birmingham City Council

Picture credits:

Paul Almasy/Corbis: 39b. Paul Baldesare/Photofusion: Posed by models: front cover. John Birdsall Photography: 32c. British Museum, London/Werner Forman Archive: 10t. BSIP, Gounot/SPL: 17t. BSIP, Laurent H. Americain/SPL: 24c. Oscar Burriel/SPL: 29b. CC Studio/SPL: 23b. Chat Magazine/Rex Features: 40c. Robert Essel NYC/Corbis: 27b. Chris Fairclough: 4, 19, 21t, 26, 41, 45. Jon Feingersh/Corbis: 8t. Peter M. Fisher/Corbis: 34b. Owen Franken/Corbis: 8b. John van Hassel/Corbis: 37t. Gary Houlder/Corbis: 12t. Jutta Klee/Corbis: 15b. Bob Krist/Corbis: 25t. Chris Lisle/Corbis: 12b. Tom & Dee Ann McCarthy/Corbis: 33b. Minnesota Historical Society/Corbis: 10b. Amet Jean Pierre/Corbis: 37b John Powell/Rex Features: 18t. Charles O'Rear/Corbis: 36c. Chuck Savage/Corbis: 25b. Isopress Senepart (SEN)/Rex Features: 31b. Shepard Sherbell/Corbis SABA: 30c. S.I.N/Corbis: 28c. Peter Turnley/Corbis: 13b. Underwood & Underwood/Corbis: 11t. Garry Watson/SPL: 22c. Michael S. Yamashita/Corbis: 35c.

The Publisher would like to thank the Brunswick Club for Young People, Fulham, London for their help with this book. Thanks to our models, including Spencer Thoroughgood, Stevie Waite and Eva Webb.

Every attempt has been made to clear copyright. Should there be any inadvertent omission, please apply to the publisher for rectification.

A CIP catalogue record for this book is available from the British Library.

Printed in Malaysia

Franklin Watts is a division of Hachette Children's Books, an Hachette UK company.

www.hachette.co.uk

Contents

What is alcohol? 8

Alcohol in the past 10

Drinking together 12

Alcohol and the body 14

Sensible drinking 16

Being drunk 18

Hangovers 20

Health risks 22

Alcoholism 24

Teenage drinking 26

Alcohol and drugs 28

The high cost of alcohol 30

Violence and crime 32

Alcohol and the law 34

Alcohol is big business 36

Alcohol and advertising 38

How to stay healthy 40

Glossary 42

Further information 43

Index 44

What is alcohol?

When people talk about alcohol they are usually referring to the alcohol in drinks. Most adults can enjoy alcohol with friends and remain healthy. However, alcohol can be addictive which means that some people come to depend on it and become ill.

Friends often enjoy a drink together. ▲

▲ Barrels of port, a type of strong wine, in a warehouse.

How is alcohol made?

Alcohol is made using a process called fermentation. To make wine, people mix grapes, water and yeast and leave them to ferment. During fermentation, the yeast feeds on the sugars in the grapes, producing alcohol. In a similar way, grains can be made into whisky, lager and beer, potatoes into vodka, honey into mead and sugar into rum.

Alcoholic drinks

Alcoholic drinks come in a wide range of flavours. Wine gets its flavour from grapes while cider tastes of apples. Alcopops taste of fruit juices or other sweet drinks.

The labels on alcoholic drinks show how strong they are. The strength is measured as the percentage of alcohol per volume. The higher the percentage number, the stronger the drink. The labels also show how many units of alcohol each drink contains (see page 16 for more on units).

Lager gets its flavour from the malt grains it is made from.

Read the labels; the vodka is the strongest drink shown here.

Your experience

"Everyone drinks, don't they? Even your aunt. It's just part of social life."
Sam, aged 18

It's your life

Alcohol affects the body in different ways. Read this book to learn the facts so that you can think about how to deal with alcohol as you grow up.

Alcohol in the past

People have drunk alcohol for thousands of years. In Europe during the medieval period, water was often too dirty to drink safely, so people drank alcohol instead.

This ancient mosaic dates from 2500 BCE and shows people drinking at a banquet.

Everyday life and religion

We know that people grew crops to make alcohol up to 7,000 years ago. In ancient China, people felt that alcohol brought happiness and wealth. In ancient Greece and Rome, wine was a popular drink. It was also used in many religious ceremonies worldwide.

Drink problems

More recently, groups of people started to blame alcohol for crime, poverty and ill-health. In the UK, the Temperance Movement started in 1832. At one point, one in ten people in the UK had joined the movement by deciding not to drink alcohol and become 'teetotal'.

American women march for Prohibition in 1917.

Police inspect illegal stores of alcohol during Prohibition.

Prohibition

In 1920, the US government introduced Prohibition in the hope of improving people's health. Prohibition meant a total ban on the making, selling and drinking of alcohol except for medical or religious use. Unfortunately, the ban led to an increase in crime. People called 'bootleggers' made a fortune by making and selling alcohol illegally. The ban actually led to people drinking more alcohol.

It's your life

Many people choose never to drink alcohol, for personal, religious or other reasons. How do you feel about being teetotal when you grow up?

Your view

Do you think the government could do anything to stop people drinking too much? What would you suggest?

Drinking together

In many countries around the world, drinking alcohol is accepted as a normal part of people's social life. Friends meet at pubs, bars and clubs and people usually serve alcohol when they hold a party.

Drinking competitions can encourage people to drink too much.

Drinking places

Drinking places vary around the world, from French bars to English pubs and Polish taverns. All are places where people meet friends, family or neighbours. Some serve food as well as alcohol, others just serve alcohol.

Many French bars serve coffee, food and alcohol.

My experience

"It sometimes feels like grown-ups can't enjoy themselves without a drink in their hands. My parents are silly when they have been drinking."

Eli, aged 10

Your view

Many pubs and bars run 'Happy Hours' where they sell alcoholic drinks at cheap prices early in the evening. They do it to attract customers but it can encourage people to drink as much as possible while the prices are low. Do you think Happy Hours should be banned?

Celebrations

All over the world, people celebrate marriages, birthdays, baptisms and other occasions with a party or a gathering. Usually people expect to be offered alcoholic drinks at these occasions.

Drinking as a group

Teenage friends often choose the same brand of drink to show their link with each other. Sometimes friends encourage each other to drink too much.

Guests enjoy a drink at a wedding.

Alcohol and the body

It takes about ten minutes for the alcohol in a drink to reach the bloodstream. Then it travels to all parts of the body.

Feeling flushed

Alcohol makes blood vessels under the skin become wider, so that blood passes through them faster and people feel warm and flushed.

Reaching the brain

The heart pumps the blood containing the alcohol around the body. In the brain it slows down the links between the brain cells and other cells. At first people may feel relaxed but gradually they may slur words together and feel dizzy or even fall over.

Your experience

"My big brother gets drunk with his friends. They act really stupid and get into trouble with the police."

Georgina, aged 13

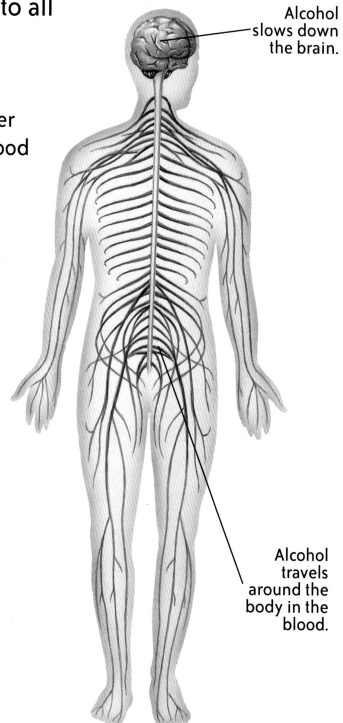

Alcohol slows down the brain.

Alcohol travels around the body in the blood.

In the kidneys

The kidneys work hard to filter out waste, including alcohol, from the blood and turns it into urine. The waste includes chemicals made by the body and also unwanted materials absorbed from food and drink.

The urine passes through the bladder. When the kidneys are dealing with alcohol, the bladder fills up quickly so people need to use the toilet more often than usual.

The kidneys pass water and waste to the bladder.

The bladder fills with urine until the person goes to the toilet.

The body has two kidneys attached to the bladder by tubes called urethras.

The hard-working liver

Some of the alcohol is taken out of the blood by the kidneys, but the rest of the job is left to the liver. This large body organ breaks down alcohol so it can be removed from the body.

It's your life

Now that you are learning about the effects of alcohol on the body, how will you behave around alcohol?

Women's bodies are not able to deal with alcohol as well as men's.

Sensible drinking

Experts agree that most adults can drink sensibly without harming their health. However, recent research suggests that there is no safe limit for young people under the age of 15.

Safe drinking levels

UK	USA	AUSTRALIA
Men:	Men:	Men:
3 or 4 units a day	2 alcoholic drinks a day	4 alcoholic drinks a day
Women:	Women:	Women:
2 or 3 units a day	1 alcoholic drink a day	2 alcoholic drinks a day

A unit of alcohol is 8 gm or 10 ml of pure alcohol, which is:
- A single measure (25 ml) of spirits
- A small glass (50 ml) of sherry or fortified wine
- A small glass (125 ml) of wine
- Half a pint of beer, cider or lager.

Government advice
The table above shows government recommendations as to how many units of alcohol it is safe to drink each day.

It's your life

Many people ignore the recommended safe drinking levels. How will you behave in the future?

Setting a limit
Many people learn how much alcohol they can drink before it starts to change their behaviour. It is recommended that people enjoy one or two alcohol-free days every week, in order to remain healthy.

▲ Doctors recommend that pregnant women do not drink any alcohol.

When to say 'no'

Sometimes it is sensible to drink no alcohol at all. Women who are pregnant (see page 23) and people who need to drive or stay alert for their jobs should not drink alcohol. Some other people should avoid alcohol, especially those with diabetes and depression.

My experience

"I make it a rule to have a soft drink or a glass of water after every alcoholic drink when I'm out with friends."

Mags, aged 19

Being drunk

If people drink more alcohol than their body can cope with, they will become drunk. Some people become more lively, others become quiet and even sad. Many feel more confident which could make them take risks.

Loss of control

Alcohol slows the brain down so people become confused and clumsy. They are more likely to fall over or have an accident. Drinking alcohol makes people more emotional. Some become happy — others become angry and violent.

Taking risks

When someone is drunk they are more likely to take risks. They might decide to walk home in the dark, do something dangerous, drink and drive or go home with a stranger.

Drinking alcohol makes most people feel relaxed and giggly.

Your experience

"At a family party I was bored and I started finishing off drinks. Soon I was being sick. I felt really embarrassed."

Sam, aged 16

Binge drinking

Some young people go out to get drunk, by drinking lots of alcohol at once. This is called binge drinking. Quite quickly they will begin to feel confused and dizzy. Then they may start to be sick, collapse on the ground or even pass out. In some cases, alcohol poisoning sets in. The drunk person needs to get medical help.

▼ Left alone, this teenager could die from alcohol poisoning.

It's your life

▶ Is drinking too much alcohol a good way to enjoy yourself? Do you need to drink alcohol to have fun?
Which is more important — meeting up with friends or drinking alcohol?

The signs of alcohol poisoning:
* fast or slow breathing
* deep sleep
* violent sickness
* cold, pale skin.

Hangovers

A hangover can make you feel sick, thirsty and have a bad headache. It is the body's way of saying you drank too much alcohol the day before.

Dark-coloured drinks, such as red wine, are more likely to cause hangovers.

Headaches and sickness

When someone drinks alcohol, their kidneys work hard to remove the alcohol from their blood (see page 15). In the process the kidneys remove a lot of water from the blood. This can lead to dehydration and a nasty headache. Alcohol also irritates the stomach and can cause sickness or diarrhoea.

Avoiding a hangover

The best way for people to avoid a hangover is not to drink too much alcohol. If someone has drunk a lot of alcohol, they can help themselves by drinking plenty of water and some fruit juice before they go to bed. The vitamin C in fruit juice helps the liver to break down alcohol. Eating a good meal or drinking a glass of milk before drinking alcohol can protect the stomach from alcohol.

Your experience

"Every time I wake up with a hangover, I think I'll never drink too much again. I've no one to blame but myself."
Kelly, aged 20

Drinking milk can slow down the rate at which the body absorbs alcohol.

Fruit juice and eggs can help the body deal with alcohol.

The liver is the large body organ just under the ribs.

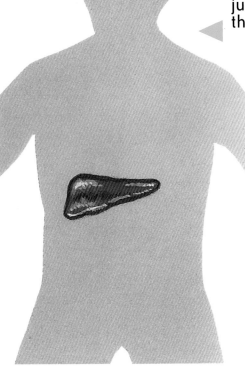

Hangover help

The best way to help cure a hangover is to drink plenty of water and fruit juice. Some people eat eggs because a chemical in the eggs helps to mop up the effects of alcohol. Painkillers can help a headache but the best thing is to rest and drink water and soft drinks.

It's your life

If you want to enjoy each day as it comes, avoid hangovers. They make people feel tired, irritated and ill and tend to last most of the day after a drinking session.

Health risks

The World Health Organisation lists drinking alcohol as one of the leading causes of death worldwide. Heavy drinking can affect almost every part of the human body, causing many problems.

Liver disease can make the skin and the eyes turn yellow.

The liver

The liver is one of the most important body organs. Without it people die. It acts like a chemical factory, cleaning up the blood. Drinking too much alcohol can damage the liver and cause liver disease.

The brain

The brain controls the body. Alcohol affects the brain cells, slowing the heart rate and breathing. After drinking too much, some people pass out and can even suffer lasting damage to the brain. Alcohol affects the memory and makes brain cells shrink

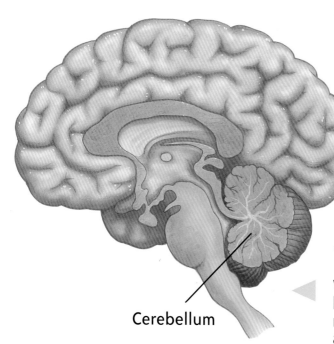

Cerebellum

When alcohol reaches the part of the brain called the cerebellum, it makes it more difficult for someone to balance and walk straight.

and die faster. It can also cause depression.

Alcohol in pregnancy

Pregnancy and alcohol do not mix. When a pregnant woman drinks alcohol, it quickly reaches her bloodstream and passes into the baby. This can damage the unborn child.

Cancer

Experts know that drinking alcohol raises a person's risk of developing seven different types of cancer. These include

cancer of the liver, bowel, mouth and breast.

The heart

Doctors continue to argue about whether some alcohol, in particular red wine, can help protect against heart disease. Research shows it helps men over the age of 40 and older women, but only if they drink no more than a glass or two a day. However drinking alcohol can also raise blood pressure and cause weight gain, leading to heart disease.

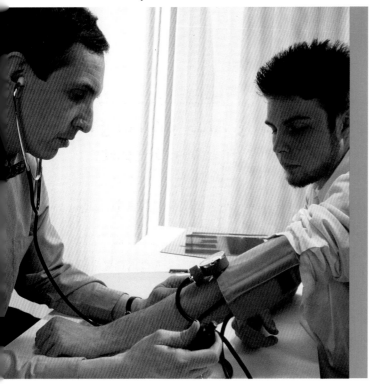

A doctor measures his patient's blood pressure.

Alcoholism

Some people become addicted to alcohol. This is called alcohol dependence, or alcoholism. Alcoholics feel as if they cannot cope without alcohol. Their drinking habit affects their health, their work and often their families.

Scientists are studying why alcoholism sometimes runs in families.

How does it happen?

Alcoholism creeps up on people. Some people use alcohol to relax. Others use it to forget their problems but they are still there when the alcohol wears off. Others may be led into drinking too much by their friends and it becomes a habit.

It's your life

We all go through tough times in our lives — times when we feel sad, lonely or confused. How will you learn to deal with these low moments? How will you avoid turning to alcohol?

Spotting the signs

It is possible for people to hide their need for alcohol. However, many alcoholics drink so much that their problem is obvious to everyone around them. When they need the next drink, almost nothing will get in their way. If they cannot have a drink, they may begin to sweat and shake.

Getting help

Some alcoholics may need medical help to stop drinking. A clinic or a hospital programme can help. Sometimes doctors give the person medicines to reduce the craving for alcohol or to help the body to cope without alcohol. A counsellor may help the alcoholic sort out some of the problems that made them turn to alcohol in the first place, such as loneliness or stress. A support group that includes people who have recovered from alcoholism can help someone recover.

Your view

As drinking alcohol and smoking can be just as dangerous to health, should there be strong warnings on alcoholic drinks, like there are on packets of cigarettes?

Many alcoholics use drink to help them escape from their problems.

Teenage drinking

Drinking alcohol has become an important part of teenage life. Young people drink with their friends at home, and out at parties, clubs and festivals.

Drinking alcohol is normal for many teenagers.

The under-15s

Recent research has shown that alcohol is very damaging to young people. The latest advice is that anyone under the age of 15 should not drink at all.

It's a fact

In most countries, it is illegal for teenagers (usually those under the age of 18 but sometimes up to the age of 21) to buy alcohol in a pub, off-licence or supermarket.

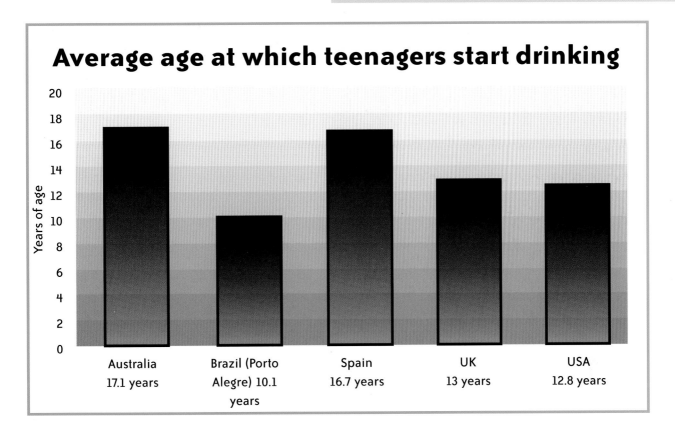

Average age at which teenagers start drinking

Years of age

Australia	Brazil (Porto Alegre)	Spain	UK	USA
17.1 years	10.1 years	16.7 years	13 years	12.8 years

Long-term effects

Some studies show that drinking too much alcohol regularly may damage young people's brains. This can make it difficult for them to study and to remember information. Doctors have also noticed a rise in the number of young people suffering from serious liver disease.

It's your life

People who drink a lot of alcohol in their early teenage years are far more likely to become an alcoholic or to develop all sorts of other problems. Will you learn to be sensible around alcohol?

More and more young women have started to drink too much, too often.

Alcohol and drugs

Alcohol, ecstasy and cocaine are all drugs. If people mix drugs together, the body can react in unexpected ways that are often harmful to their health.

Clubbers sometimes take drugs and drink alcohol, a very dangerous mixture.

Mixing drugs

Alcohol can make some drugs stronger; it can also stop other drugs from working properly, including medicines. Alcohol is known to interact with over 150 other kinds of drug, sometimes causing illness, injury and death.

Recreational drugs

Alcohol is a recreational drug that people drink to help them enjoy themselves. Some people think that drinking alcohol can encourage people to try out other recreational drugs that are illegal, such as ecstasy and cocaine. Mixing alcohol with these drugs can be very dangerous, even deadly. Mixing drugs can also cause long-term problems such as confusion and memory loss.

▲ Alcohol and medicine don't mix. Keep to water.

Your view

Some people think it is unfair that drugs such as heroin or cocaine are illegal, while alcohol isn't. Do you think that alcohol should be treated the same as other addictive drugs? Do you think there is any difference between drugs and alcohol?

Alcohol and medicines

Alcohol makes some medicines stronger, including sleeping pills, tranquillisers, anti-depressants and some painkillers. It can also stop antibiotics from working properly, putting health at risk, and cause sickness. It is best not to drink alcohol if you are taking any medicines.

It's your life

The laws on alcohol can be confusing.

It is not an illegal drug but it is illegal for someone under the age of 18 to be sold alcohol. It is also illegal to buy alcohol for someone under the age of 18.

The high cost of alcohol

Each year governments spend a huge amount of money helping people who are suffering from alcohol-related diseases or whose lives have been ruined by alcohol.

Thousands of injuries each year are related to alcohol.

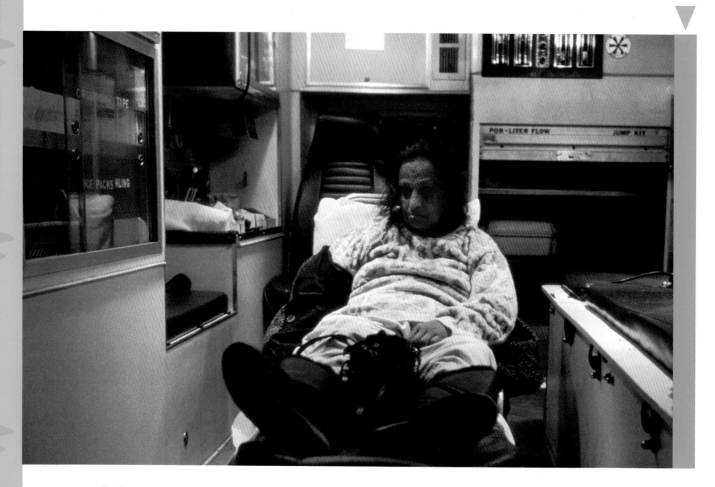

Health costs

Alcohol-related illnesses and injuries cost health services billions of pounds each year. The injuries are caused by drunken fights, road accidents linked to drink-driving and accidents at home. Then there is the cost of treating diseases caused by drinking alcohol, from liver disease, to cancer to illnesses such as depression.

Employment costs

Millions of working days are lost each year because workers have a hangover or an alcohol-related illness. Someone who was drunk the night before is more likely to have an accident at work.

Unhappy lives

Living with parents who drink too much can be misery for children. They are often neglected and may need extra support from outside the family. Schoolchildren who drink are unlikely to do well at school. Alcoholism often leads to family break-up, job loss, poverty and to people becoming homeless.

Your experience

"My sister works in an Accident and Emergency department. She sees kids who've passed out because they've drunk so much, and others who are really badly hurt because they've been in an alcohol-related fight."

Mel, aged 15

It's your life

If someone close to you is drinking too much, ask a trusted adult for help. A trusted adult could be a parent, grandparent, adult friend or a teacher.

Many alcoholics become homeless.

31

Violence and crime

Police figures suggest that alcohol is involved in half of all crimes. Often these crimes relate to drink-driving or to the licensing laws — such as selling or serving alcohol to under-age drinkers. Drinking alcohol can also make some people more likely to commit violent crimes.

Young men often get into fights when they are drunk.

Bad behaviour

Young men can often become angry and even violent when they have been drinking a lot of alcohol. A quarter of all teenage boys get into a fight after they have been drinking, leading to trouble with the police.

Your experience

"My brother was out for the night with his friends. They were walking home, minding their own business, when some young men picked a fight with them. My brother ended up needing stitches."

Luke, aged 12

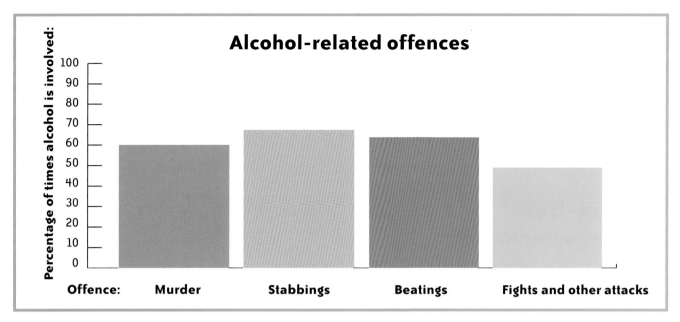

Alcohol-related offences

Percentage of times alcohol is involved:

100
90
80
70
60
50
40
30
20
10
0

| Offence: | Murder | Stabbings | Beatings | Fights and other attacks |

Hot spots

Many fights break out in city centres after pubs and night-clubs close. Drinking too much is blamed for rising levels of crime, especially among young people. Some countries ban alcohol at sporting events to prevent trouble breaking out.

Violent crime

Studies in the US show that drinking alcohol is more likely to lead to violent crime than any other drug. People find it more difficult to control their emotions once they have been drinking. Violence in the home often occurs after drinking.

Drinking too much can lead to violence in the home. ▶

It's your life

Young people who drink a lot of alcohol are far more likely to be involved in crime or be the victims of crime.

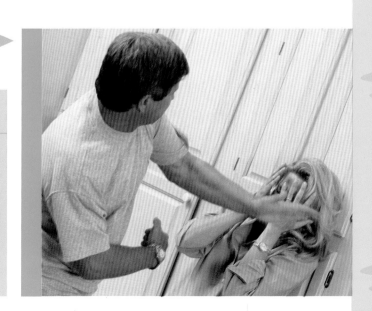

Alcohol and the law

Governments use laws to control the making, selling and drinking of alcohol.

Muslim men drink coffee with friends in a café in India.

Alcohol-free

There are a number of countries, including Saudi Arabia, Qatar, Kuwait, Pakistan and parts of India, where alcohol is forbidden or strictly controlled. This is because most people in these countries are Muslim, and follow a religion that bans alcohol.

Some pubs and nightclubs use door staff to stop under-age drinkers from being allowed in.

The law

Even in countries where people are allowed to drink alcohol, the governments use laws to control the drinking and selling of alcohol. Special licences are needed for all places selling alcohol. These control when, where and to whom the alcohol can be sold or consumed. It is against the law to sell alcohol to people under a certain age — this varies from country to country.

Your experience

"When my parents go out with friends, they share a taxi. They won't drink and drive."

Kieran, aged 13

Police powers

In many countries, the police can arrest and charge anyone who is 'drunk and disorderly' in a public place. They may also be allowed to take away alcohol from anyone under the age of 18 or even 21. Some countries ban drink-driving. Others set a limit for the amount of alcohol a driver can have in their blood.

▲ A police officer in Germany asks a driver to breathe into a breathalyser.

It's your life

Alcohol slows down the body's reactions so drinking and driving cars can be very dangerous. The law varies around the world but many people argue that no one should drink and drive.

Alcohol is big business

Alcohol today is big business. The alcohol industry makes billions of pounds a year, employs millions of people and even raises money for governments.

Wine bottles in a bottling factory.

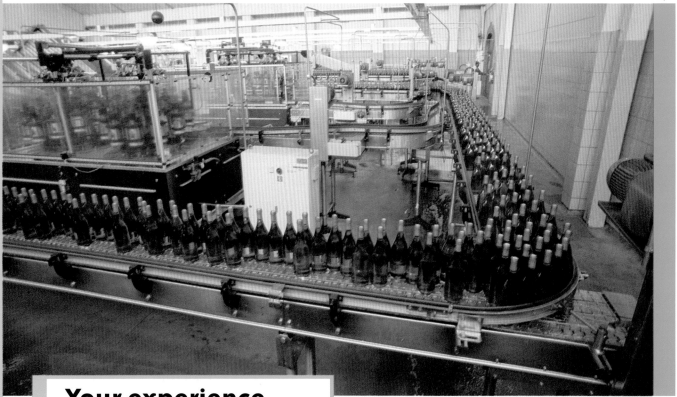

Your experience

"I've been abroad a few times with my family. Wherever we go, my dad is able to buy his favourite type of beer, even if we are thousands of miles from home!"

Matt, aged 16

The alcohol industry

Wine-makers, distillers, brewers, off-licences, supermarkets, pubs, bars and nightclubs — the alcohol industry is vast. They do encourage sensible drinking but they don't want to stop people drinking alcohol.

Multinationals

Recently, a few huge companies, known as multinationals, have taken control of the alcohol market, especially for beers and spirits. It is often possible to drink the same brands of alcoholic drink in countries all around the world.

An advert for beer in China.

Your view

Should governments force the alcohol industry to charge more for alcoholic drinks? Would this stop young people from drinking too much? What do you think would help?

Taxes on alcohol

Many governments around the world use taxes and duties on alcohol to raise money for their countries. Taxes can also be used to try to control how much people drink by making alcohol expensive. Some of the money raised by taxing alcohol is then spent fixing the problems alcohol causes.

Taxes on alcohol in France are lower than in some other European countries.

Alcohol and advertising

The alcohol industry spends billions of pounds each year advertising alcoholic drinks.

The alcohol industry targets young people, as shown here.

Lifestyle adverts

Alcohol advertisements often show attractive young people drinking and having fun in glamorous places. Successful adverts can result in far more people choosing to drink a particular type of drink.

Targeting the young

To alcohol companies, young people are the drinkers of the future. They often use websites packed with games and competitions to encourage young drinkers to choose their particular brand of alcoholic drink.

The alcohol industry uses the four 'Ps' when marketing alcohol to young people:

- **Products** — alcopops and drinks that appeal to young drinkers
- **Promotions** — in teen magazines, and by showing products in films
- **Places** — opening bars in student and low-income areas
- **Prices** — some beers are now as cheap as soft drinks or bottled water.

Codes of practice

In many countries, governments set out rules and guidance in the form of codes of practice about alcohol advertising. Some people believe that advertisers regularly ignore the codes and that there should be more restrictions in this area and in sports sponsorship.

It's your view

Do you think advertising encourages people to drink more, or to try a different brand of alcohol? Do you take any notice of advertising?

Your experience

"It's confusing. Parents tell you not to drink, then you see all these cool people in adverts drinking and having fun."

Kate, aged 18

Safe drinking messages

Some adverts warn against the dangers of drink-driving. Perhaps more money should be spent on adverts that give messages about safe drinking, including the dangers of binge drinking.

▼ A French advertisement warns against the dangers of drink-driving.

jamais d'alcool au volant

(This sign says: "Never drink and drive.")

DELEGATION A LA SECURITE ROUTIERE et LA PREVENTION ROUTIERE

How to stay healthy

As we grow up, we learn how to care for ourselves. We learn about eating healthily, taking enough exercise, using our talents and how to stay safe. This includes staying safe around alcohol.

A choice

Some people decide not to drink alcohol at all. Others drink sensibly with friends and it helps them relax and have fun.

It's your life

Drinking alcohol can make someone feel happy at first. But alcohol is a depressant, a drug that can leave someone feeling low and slows them down. How can that be fun?

Alcohol doesn't solve problems — it just creates more.

A way of life

Young people learn from what is going on around them. In countries such as France and Italy, many parents give their children small amounts of alcoholic drinks with the family meal. Research shows that these countries have less alcohol-related problems.

Simple rules

If people do drink alcohol regularly, they can stay healthy by following these simple rules: find ways to have fun without alcohol; don't drink every day; and never drink alone.

Watch for signs

If you can't enjoy yourself without a drink in your hand, or you are drinking alone, seek help from a counsellor, doctor or helpline (see page 43).

Top tips

Stay off all alcohol until you are at least 15.

If you are drinking between the ages of 15 and 17, it should only be once a week, if at all.

After that, learn to drink sensibly.

Never drink alone.

When you go drinking with friends, look after each other and make sure that you all get home safely.

A good night out

People meet to go to the cinema, play sports together or just chat. A good night out is one where you are having fun.

▼ Friends can have fun without alcohol.

41

Glossary

Addictive drug: a drug that the body and mind can become dependent on.

Binge drinking: drinking heavily in a short period of time.

Blood pressure: the pressure of blood pressing against the blood vessels as it flows around the body.

Bloodstream: the blood circulating within the body.

Body organ: part of the body that performs an important job, such as the heart, lungs, liver or kidneys.

Breathalyser: a small device for measuring the level of alcohol in the blood through a breath sample.

Cell: a tiny unit of living material.

Cocaine: an addictive recreational drug.

Dehydrate: to dry out.

Depression: a sad or low state of mind when people lose interest in everything and feel hopeless.

Distiller: someone who makes alcoholic spirits (gin, vodka etc).

Ecstasy: a recreational drug that produces happy feelings.

Fermentation: the process in which yeast works with sugars in fruit or grain to make alcohol and carbon dioxide.

Illegal: against the law.

Liver disease: general term for several health conditions which cause the liver cells to die.

Liver transplant: transfer a liver from someone who has died to someone whose liver is diseased.

Mead: an alcoholic drink made from honey and water.

Medieval: the period in European history from roughly 1150 to 1450.

Off-licence: a shop where alcoholic drinks may be bought to be drunk elsewhere.

Prohibition: a total ban, in particular the ban on making or selling alcohol in the US during the 1920s.

Recreational drug: a drug someone takes to help them enjoy themselves.

Spirits: strong types of alcoholic drink, including whisky and vodka.

Teetotal: Somebody who never drinks alcohol.

Temperance: giving up alcohol.

Under-age drinker: someone under the legal age to be drinking alcohol.

Unit of alcohol: 8 gms or 10 ml of pure alcohol.

Yeast: tiny fungi used to make alcohol through fermentation.

Further information

UNITED KINGDOM

Alcohol Concern
A national agency concerned with alcohol misuse.
www.alcoholconcern.org.uk/

Childline
Childline is a free, confidential helpline for young people.
www.childline.org.uk/pages/ info.aspx

Drinkaware
An organisation set up to increase people's understanding of the role of alcohol in society.
www.drinkaware.co.uk/

Talk to Frank
A national drugs and alcohol awareness site for young people.
www.talktofrank.com/

AUSTRALIA

Australian Drug Information Network
Provides links to Internet sites in Australia and elsewhere that have useful information on alcohol and other drugs.
www.adin.com.au/

Children's Youth and Women's Health Service (South Australia)
Click on 'Nearly Teens' and then on 'Alcohol – it can affect your life'.
www.cyh.com/SubDefault.aspx?p=2 55

Reach Out
Provides much information about issues that affect young people.
http://au.reachout.com/find/issues/ alcohol-other-drugs/alcohol

Note to parents and teachers: Every effort has been made by the Publishers to ensure that these websites are suitable for children, that they are of the highest educational value, and that they contain no inappropriate or offensive material. However, because of the nature of the Internet, it is impossible to guarantee that the contents of these sites will not be altered. We strongly advise that Internet access is supervised by a responsible adult.

Index

addiction 8, 24, 25, 29, 42
advertising 37, 38-39
alcohol,
  history of 10-11
  how it's made 8
alcohol dependence 8, 24-25
alcohol industry 36-39
alcohol poisoning 19
alcoholics 24, 25, 27, 31
alcoholism 24-25, 31
alcopops 9, 38

bars 12, 13, 36
beer 8, 16, 36, 37, 38
binge drinking 19, 39, 42
blood pressure 23, 42
brain 14, 18, 22, 23, 27

cancer 23, 30
celebrations 12, 13
cider 9, 16
cocaine 28, 29, 42
crime 10, 11, 31, 32-33

depression 17, 23, 30, 42
drink-driving 17, 30, 32, 35, 39
drugs 28-29, 33, 40, 42
drunkenness 14, 18-19, 31

ecstasy 28, 29, 42

fermentation 8, 42

hangovers 20-21, 31
Happy Hours 13
heart 14, 22, 23, 42

kidneys 15, 20, 42

labelling of drinks 9
lager 8, 9, 16
law and alcohol 26, 29, 32, 34-35
liver 15, 20, 21, 22, 23, 27, 30, 42

mead 8, 42
medicines 25, 28, 29

nightclubs 12, 26, 28, 33, 34, 36

off-licences 26, 36, 42

pregnancy 17, 23
pricing of drinks 13, 37, 38
Prohibition 10, 11, 42
pubs 12, 13, 26, 33, 34, 36

recreational drugs 28, 29, 42
religion 10, 11, 34
rum 8

safe drinking levels 16
social life 8, 9, 10-11, 12-13, 19, 26, 40, 41
spirits 16, 37, 42

taxes on alcohol 37
teenagers 13, 19, 26-27, 32, 33, 34, 38
teetotal 10, 11, 42
Temperance Movement 10, 42

units of alcohol 9, 16, 42

vodka 8, 9, 42
violence 18, 30, 31, 32-33

whisky 8, 42
wine 8, 9, 16, 20, 23, 36